SAY WHAT YOU WANT

Copyright 2009 by: Ale

ISBN: 978-0-9562935-0-3

Published in the United Kingdom by:

**The Light Academy Publishing House
In association with She Story Publications**

For further information or permission, address:

The Light Academy Publishing House

19-21 Thames Rd, Barking, Essex, London, IG11 0HN, United Kingdom

Tel: +447903799998

Or reach us on the Internet:

http://www.vpa-tv.org

E-mail:vpacanaanland@yahoo.co.uk; vpateam@googlemail.com

Unless otherwise stated all scripture text used in this book are taken
from the King James Version of the Bible.

TABLE OF CONTENTS

Preface

Many people do not realize the power in the words they speak. There is something about spoken words that goes beyond the natural realm. Our words contribute in setting the pace for our experiences in life. Our words set the stage for the events of our lives but many people do not seem to realize that.

Where you are today is a product of the words that you have spoken about your life in the past. When you say you can not, you rob yourself of the ability to perform. When you say you do not have what you need to achieve certain things in your life, you push away those things from coming to you.

When you are busy talking about your troubles and challenges, you multiply them, but when you talk about the solutions, you hasten the arrival of your victory.

Jesus said that we shall have what we say and in this book I have endeavoured by the help of the blessed Holy Spirit to explain how that works. This is a revised edition. The first edition was a great blessing to so many people that I decided to update and improve on it. This time I added prayers at the end of each chapter. I call these ACTION PRAYERS. These powerful prayer points are to be prayed with seriousness and force so that the reader will actually take in the anointing behind the message and be able to practically walk in victory by the right use of the tongue.

As you read this powerful book, keep in mind that you will eventually get what you say by faith and so it is better to say what you want rather than spending most of your precious time talking about the things you do not want. As you read I pray that the anointing of the Holy Spirit will come upon your tongue and assist you to stay in perpetual victory as you SAY WHAT YOU WANT BY FAITH.

PASTOR ALEX OMOKUDU

CHAPTER 1

BITS AND HORSES

GOD'S WORD

The Lord has shown us in His word all we need to know in order to be able to live fulfilling lives in accordance with His divine will. Even though God has given us all the information that we need, it is very obvious that most people live their lives as though such information is not available.

We need to be willing to know what God has documented in His word for our benefit. The power of knowing the truth cannot be over emphasized. Many times the Bible declares the danger of either not knowing or neglecting the truth of scriptures. Many today are perishing for lack of knowledge as the word stated in Hosea 4:6:

> **"My people are destroyed for lack of knowledge: because thou hast rejected knowledge, I will also reject thee, that thou shalt be no priest to me: seeing thou hast forgotten the law of thy God, I will also forget thy children."**

When we neglect or reject the truth of God's word the consequence results in a negative situation that make things appear as if God has rejected us. Many times people go through unpleasant experiences and it seems as if God has rejected or forsaken them. At such times it is very normal for us to try to blame it on somebody else or something else and at times even upon God Himself.

The truth however is that when we neglect or ignore the word of God, we put ourselves into situations that make it seem as if God has rejected us. God does not forget nor reject His children as long as they are working in the light of His word that He has made available to them.

Even though mothers can hardly forget their babies, God clearly teaches us in Isaiah 49:15 that even if some mothers do forget their babies, He will never forget His own children.

"Can a woman forget her sucking child, that she should not have compassion on the son of her womb? yea, they may forget, yet will I not forget thee."

He has all of them engraved upon the palm of His mighty hand. He has our interest at heart all the time and whether we feel like He has forgotten us or not, He has promised never to forget us and His word is true and faithful.

When it seems as though God has forgotten us it is likely that we have not walked in the light of His truth as revealed in His word. This is not always the case but it is clear from the word of God that it is a clear possibility. We could be walking in all the light that we have and yet feel as though God has forgotten us, this is real and can happen; at such times we are to stick to the word of God that we have with unyielding faith without giving up.

Isaiah 50:10 "Who is among you that feareth the LORD that obeyeth the voice of his servant that walketh in darkness, and hath no light? Let him trust in the name of the LORD, and stay upon his God."

When you do all you know to do and you walk in all the light you have and yet still experience some measure of darkness, all you can do is to go ahead and still trust in the Lord and remain faithful to Him and His word. You must continue to trust in the Lord even when you think you ought to give up. Giving up is not an option. When we have done all that we know we are supposed to do we must stand and continue to stand as Paul said in Ephesians 6:13

"Wherefore take unto you the whole armour of God that ye may be able to withstand in the evil day, and having done all to stand".

For us to be sure that the apparent darkness and the seeming absence of God in our affairs is not caused by our neglect of the word of God we need to be sure that we take the issue of God's word very seriously. We need to know what the word of God has to say to us on any and every issue of life. God has promised not to forget us and that includes His release of grace and compassion upon us without end.

Sadly enough however, some do not even take time to study their Bibles to see what God has to say to them concerning the issues of life. Some Christians listen to sermon after sermon and yet there does not seem to be any drastic change in their attitude to life and sad to say, many still live their lives the way the ungodly people do. To such half hearted Christians the following psalm does not really apply.

> **"Blessed is the man that walketh not in the counsel of the ungodly, nor standeth in the way of sinners nor sitteth in the seat of the scornful. But his delight is in the law of the Lord, and in his law doth he meditate day and night." Ps.1:1-2.**

Since they walk in the counsel of the ungodly, stand in the way of sinners and sit in the seat of the scornful, they naturally do not have a consuming delight for the word of God therefore they do not meditate on it day and night, and consequently they are not really blessed in life.

We can not be consumed with the affairs and ways of the world if we must be on fire for God. Our hearts can not be running after the world and its ways of sin and then have a passion for God and His word at the same time. The blessedness that belongs to those who meditate day and night on the word of God is not available to those Christians who are all consumed with worldly things.

There needs to be a measure of separation from the world if we must have a heart that is ready to meditate on the word of God as a habit. We cannot eat our cake and have it at the same time. Believers who are spending so much time watching Television, visiting people without any purpose and wasting precious time in non-destiny helping issues get cheated of the blessedness that belongs to the righteous.

We need to get a revelation of how much our Father loves us and is concerned about the issues of our lives. This revelation will affect how we relate to God as His children and consequently how we relate to ourselves and situations in lives.

I believe it is the display of the loving Fatherhood of God that has caused Him to make all that we need available to us through Christ Jesus. He has done all that He will do for now. It is up to us to discover what He has provided for us and also the principles that He has ordained for the operation of the things of His kingdom. Any person who understands the Bible will readily realize that God is a 'man of principles'. He sets out the principles and expects His people to walk in them so that He will be able to play His part.

EQUAL LOVE FOR ALL

Every parent can understand when I say that some children are easier to love than others. Some children do the things that are right while some others seem to be overtly interested in doing wrong things ever so often. As a result of this it is natural for parents to find themselves loving some children more than they do others. Children that are very obedient and respectful naturally attract the love of their parents more than those who are unruly and perpetual lawbreakers.

Even though this type of propensity exists in almost every natural family, parents must always do all they can to resist this discriminatory love towards their children. However, the truth is that such a tendency is there with us as human beings.

Very different from us, God our Father loves all of us equally. God is the only Father who has no favorite children; **He loves all of His dear children with the same love**. When I talk about the children of God I mean all who are free from sin by the blood of Jesus Christ having been born from above not by the will of man, or of the flesh but of God.

I am not talking about those who attend church but do not have a dynamic personal relationship with the Lord Jesus Christ. Too many people are just out to play church, they do not really know the God they profess, and they are just members of a church congregation but not members of the kingdom of God.

> **John 1:12-13"But as many as received him, to them gave he power to become the sons of God, even to them that believe on his name: 13 Which were born, not of blood, nor of the will of the flesh, nor of the will of man, but of God."**

Our new birth experience is God's idea and not ours. He is the initiator of our born again new life. He authored our new life and He loves all of us in the same way. God loves the world renowned evangelist who has preached in one hundred countries just the same way as He loves the old woman in the village who got saved two weeks ago.

This is not to suggest that God does not love the sinners. He loves the sinners with such passion that He gave His blessed Son to die for them.

John 3:16 "For God so love the world that he gaveth His only begotten son, that whosoever believeth in him, should not die but have everlasting life."

Before we became saved we were all sinners and yet He loved us and saved us from our many sins, so we know that He loves even the sinners. However, I am addressing the issue of God's love for His children.

Whether you are an apostle, prophet, or an usher, He loves you with the same love. Whether you often fall into sin or walk in holiness all the time, He loves you the same way. Whether you are very talented or just managing to get by spiritually, He loves you all the same. Whether you are a famous bible scholar or you just know only a few scriptures, your heavenly Father loves you the same way He loves any child of His.

This is one of the great wonders of our Father's amazing love for all of His children. Like I stated earlier, this is not to say that God does not love the sinners who are wallowing in their sinful ways, He loves them but they do not have the type of access that the child of God has to this love until they come into fellowship with God and His Son Jesus Christ.

It is clear that John 3:16 is a direct reference to sinners, so we have proof that God loves all sinners but it is when they respond to that love and come to Christ that they enter into the realm of conscious experience of that love. Many sinners are in hell today not because God never loved them, He did love them and still does but they never accessed that love because they did not accept Jesus into their lives as Lord and Savior.

God loves all of His children the same way but the wonder of God's infinite Love, is that He loves you the same way He loves JESUS CHRIST His holy son, and He couldn't possibly love you more than that. The Father loves you just like He loves Jesus Christ our Lord (JN 17:23) which love can measure up to that? NONE!

John 17:23 "I in them, and thou in me, that they may be made perfect in one; and that the world may know that thou hast sent me, and hast loved them, as thou hast loved me."

The Father loves us with an everlasting and infinite love. When believers get a working revelation of this love that God has for all of us, it opens them up for encounters with God that propel them to the realm where they begin to enjoy all that God has planned for them. As a result of the Father's love for us He has made available to us all things that we need, both for our natural lives as human beings and for our spiritual lives as children of God who is called 'the Father of spirits' (Heb. 12:9). He is committed to our physical life as well as our spiritual lives. His Fatherhood covers all areas of our lives and we can enjoy His care and grace in all areas.

ALL THINGS ARE READY

The principles of God's kingdom are the keys that give us access into the blessings that he has made available to us, but when we do not know these principles we suffer lack in the midst of plenty. We suffer like the prodigal son, feeding among swine as it were, while our precious Heavenly Father has an unlimited supply of all that we shall ever need in this life and the next. Our Father has more than we shall ever need both in this life and in that which is to come and He is ready to shower His great blessings upon us. There is no area of our lives that is not covered by the provisions that God has made. He is concerned about every area of our lives and His love reaches out to us in every sphere of existence.

Are you in need of spiritual power to do the work of God, to live a holy and very prayerful life? Are you in need of more grace to serve God more fruitfully? Do you need healing for your body and a lifestyle of permanent good health? Do you need financial miracles? Do you need God's intervention in your business or your job? Do you need God's intervention in your marriage or in your need for a spouse? Do you need the spirit of revelation to move higher and higher in the knowledge of God and His word?

Do you need divine protection? What do you want? As a servant of God I declare to you in the mighty name of Jesus Christ the Son of the living God, that He has made all these available for you, all you need is to know the principles He has ordained for you to walk in to be able to enjoy them.

Apostle Peter made this clear in one of his epistles. God has made provision for us in both the natural realm and the spiritual realm. It is important to know that God is not only interested in our spiritual lives, but that He is very much interested in our physical natural lives as well. He is interested in our relationships, He is interested in our families, and He is interested in our jobs and businesses and in all that concerns us.

2 Peter 1.3 "According as his divine power hath given unto us all things that pertain unto life and godliness, through the knowledge of him that hath called us to glory and virtue:"

God has not called His people into a life of shame and reproach but to a life of glory and virtue. Honour is our portion as God's people and one of the ways of actualizing that is through the knowledge of the principles of God's word that enable us to gain access to all things that God has given to us, things that pertain to life and godliness. The principles of God's word are unchanging because the word of God is eternally abiding. When we access these unchanging principles we are sure to tap into the benefits that they carry.

119:89-90. "For ever, O LORD, thy word is settled in heaven. Thy faithfulness is unto all generations: thou hast established the earth, and it abideth."

Since these principles are based on God's unchanging and ever abiding word, they are sure to work for ever. They draw their strength from the infallible word of God and the infallibility of the word of God guarantees their continuous workability.

Matthew 24:35 "Heaven and earth shall pass away, but my words shall not pass away."

Every word of God is a covenant in making from the very moment God spoke it, but actually becomes a covenant when we respond to it the way God intended us to. He becomes committed by covenant to perform that word. Once God becomes committed it is as good as done. When God becomes committed nothing can defeat His purpose; He is God and He rules over all. No matter how His purpose seems to be failing it will never fail because He will stick to His word to the very end.

Psalm 89:34 "My covenant will I not break, nor alter the thing that is gone out of my lips."

Once God has spoken the word it enters the realm of covenant made real by our proper response **based on God's terms**. Therefore principles based on the clear word of God become covenanted to deliver because God is personally committed to them.

In this book, I am led of the Holy Spirit to share one of these principles of God's kingdom with you and as you read, read prayerfully because God is about to change your entire life. There are a number of principles in the word of God and when you are able to catch any of them you come into a new realm, a realm where that principle gives you an opening into the dimension of blessing.

This is a principle that runs across many other principles. When you are able to get the revelation of this principle you will have a new realm of experience in your life. This principle affects all areas of our lives and so it's vital that you engage in it very consciously. This very important principle is **SAY WHAT YOU WANT**.

This vital principle is absolutely based on the word of God, so it is a constant. It is centered on the power of the tongue and the fact that the right or wrong use of the tongue has undeniable consequences in the lives of people. That means you and I can not afford to say whatever we like to say and get away with it, we can not say just anything we hear others say and be unaffected by it, we can not just keep saying whatever we feel like saying and yet be unaffected by those words. Our words affect us in ways beyond our imagination.

The right use of our tongue goes a long way in procuring the fullness of our destinies in God. What we say and continue to say will have great repercussions on our experiences. This is a very vital principle in the word of the Lord. In this book, I seek by the help of God to look at this biblical principle and to make it plainer to us and show how we can use it for our benefit and not to our hurt. When well used, we gain but when wrongly used we lose, but I decree that as you read this book you will never be a loser any more in Jesus name.

The major text that I am using for this study is James 3:3-5:

> **"Behold we put bits in the horses' mouths, that they may obey us; and we turn about their whole body. Behold also the ship, which though they be so great, and are driven of fierce winds, yet they are turn about with a very small helm, withersoever the governor listeth. Even so the tongue…"**

As a child of God, the chances are that you have read this scripture many times, but I suggest that you pay close attention to the great truths that the Holy Spirit will be sharing with us in this in-depth study.

The Strength of the Horse

In the above scripture the Holy Spirit compares the tongue to two things:

1. The bits used for horses.
2. The helm used for ships.

We all know that horses are strong animals capable of running long distances without being tired. When you talk of 'raw strength' horses are much stronger than human beings. Horses are animals of great strength that is why they were used for war in bible days. Not only are horses strong but bold, that accounts for why they are the only animals used as vehicles of war, horses are strong in battle, fearless and self confident.

During the time of Job's trials, he uttered some statements that made God come to him with incredible questions. God wanted Job to know that before the almighty he was like nothing. From the question He asked Job about the horse, we discover some very interesting things about the strength and boldness of this animal of war.

Job. 39:19-25 "Hast thou given the horse strength? Cansth thou make him afraid as grasshopper? The glory of his nostril is terrible. He paveth in the valley, and rejoiceth in his strength: he goeth on to meet the armed men. He mocketh at fear and is not affrighted; neither turneth he back from sword. The quiver raffles against him, the glittering spear and the shield. He swallowed the ground with fierceness and rage neither believeth he that it is the sound of the trumpets, Ha-ha; and he smelleth the battle afar of, the thunder of the captains and the shoutings."

The Hebrew word for strength used for the horse here is the word "gheb-oo-raw" and it means strength, might, valour, bravery, mighty deeds. Horses are very powerful. They are full of valour and mighty deeds. Where other animals run out of strength the horse maintains power and vigour. Horses are also very bold, nothing makes them to be afraid, and they are not like the grasshoppers who are easily scared. Their bravery is awesome that they actually mock at fear.

No battlefield is so tough that they will not dare it. What a powerful animal the horse is; strong, bold and fearless. When the bible said that the horse smells the battle afar off, the Hebrew word for smell is ruwach {roo'-akh} and does not only mean to smell, scent, perceive odour, but it also means to accept and to have delight in.

That means that the horse has delight in battle and actually accepts it whenever it comes. The horse never cringes back from war, he actually accepts it. The amazing thought I want to share with you is that despite the awesome strength and great boldness of the horse, man is able to control it.

Man is able to bring this strong animal under control, making it obey him and making it go whichever direction he chooses. Even if the horse wants to go east, the rider can make it to go west if he so desires. If the horse wants to run fast, the rider can make it run slow if he so desires. If the horse wants to stop running the rider can decide otherwise and make it continue running for as long as he wants. If the rider decides that the horse should stop running and start walking he can make it do just that.

The way man controls this animal is not by tying a rope to its leg and pulling that rope, it's not by putting on iron chain on its neck. It's not by holding the tail; it's not by putting its head inside a cage. It's not by blinding its eyes; it's not by breaking one of its legs. NO! NO! NO! None of the above will ever bring the horse under control in fact any of these will make the horse release its self-will and anger.

Even if you were to try to make the horse move where you want by doing any of the things just mentioned, you will not be able to get it to obey you. The anger of the Horse is stirred up when you try to control it in the wrong way. We must look at the correct way for controlling the horse. Inside the truth about the control of the horse we shall find the wonder of controlling our own lives the way God intended. If the horse can be controlled then our situations can be controlled. If the horse can be controlled then our circumstances can be controlled. If the horse can be controlled then our lives can be controlled.

THE POWER OF BITS

The horse is so self-willed and strong that you can't even force it to drink water, that is why we have the saying "you can force a horse to the river but you can never force it to drink water". As important and good as water drinking is, you can not force the horse to drink water.

The scripture tells us that the only way to get this powerful animal to obey us is to do something to it's MOUTH; BITS, BITS, BITS. That is the word, 'bits'. The moment you put bits in the horse's mouth you gain dominion over it, it begins to obey you and only then shall you be able to turn around its whole body, the head, the legs, the tail etc.

James 3:5 says "Even so the tongue….." I lay emphasis on the statement: **'even so the tongue'**. The horse is very powerful but when you are able to put the bits in its mouth you are in charge.

YOUR TONGUE CONTROLS YOUR LIFE

It is your tongue that controls your whole life. Your tongue controls your health; your finances, your spiritual life, your family, your business, essentially, your tongue controls the entirety of your life. The Bible says "even so the tongue".

Whenever the rider of the horse wants it to change direction all he needs to do is to change the direction of the bits. When you discover that your life is going in a wrong direction and you desire a change to the positive direction simply change the 'bit's direction' turn your tongue. If you want to change the downward direction that your business is heading, change the direction of your tongue.

If you want a change in the direction of your finances, turn your tongue to the desired direction, say what you want. If your spiritual life is tending towards backsliding and you find yourself praying less than usual; you're beginning to love the world, replacing godliness with worldliness; then as a matter of urgency change the direction of your bits, turn your tongue. To see desired changes in your life, you need to be willing to make a change in the use of your tongue. What are you saying? What is coming out of your mouth?

Turn your tongue to the direction you want your life to take. This is very important. As the horse rider turns the bits to the direction he or she wants the horse to face, in the same way it is our responsibility to turn our tongues to the direction we want our lives to face and as our tongues remain in that direction, not very long, our lives will follow in that same route.

Whenever the horse rider turns the bit in the horse's mouth, the horse automatically changes direction. The horse rider does not need to beg the horse and he does not need to begin to wish all day that the horse would face a particular direction; all he needs is to simply turn the bit to the desired direction. There are many people who wish all day that their finances would change. Some wish that their spiritual life would change but yet nothing significant happens to them in the form of change.

Wishing is not the answer. The answer is in turning the direction of your tongue to your desired destination. The Bible says, "even so the tongue…" the tongue is like the horse's bits, if you turn the bit left the horse will go left, if you turn it to the right the horse will go right; if you want your life to go left, turn your tongue left; if you want your life to turn right, turn your tongue to the right. The key is **SAY WHAT YOU WANT**.

Many people never get what they want because they are always busy saying what **they do not want**. This is a very significant issue on the subject of the correct use of the tongue. When you are busy talking about what you do not want, you are setting up yourself to get the things that you do not want in your life. Some people are always talking about sickness and then they wonder why they are often sick. If you are always talking about the hardness of life, you are programming your self for a hard life.

When people in a difficult situation focus on talking about the negative situation they are in, they set themselves up to experience the things they do not really want. People who take delight in talking about fearful and evil things set themselves up for a life of fear and the evil that comes with it.

Take it this way, if you are in a financial situation that is not good, you do not need to keep talking about how hard things are. How you do not seem to have the money to do the things you need to do, how money seems to be running away from you and so on. It is a fact that you do not have money right now, but that does not mean that you have to keep talking about it all the time. If you are always talking about how you do not have money, you are programming yourself to be that way and to stay without money.

The fact that you are sick does not mean that you should turn the sickness into a song you sing all day and all night. Even if you feel terrible in your body, you do not have to keep talking about the pains and how your body is feeling very bad. The truth is that you can afford to keep your self from talking about the sickness.

Some people are always looking for somebody to show them pity and so they focus on talking about the negatives in their lives to draw the self pity they are looking for. When you are facing a challenge in your health for example you do not need somebody to be telling you sorry. That is not what will get you well so do not continue to talk about the sickness in order to gain self pity.

If you do not know what to say except to glorify the sickness then I advise that you keep your mouth shut. Watch what you are saying with your mouth. Instead of talking about sickness why not talk about sound health and divine healing? Why not talk about the power of God to heal? Talk about the grace of God to set you free.

We live in an evil world and that is the truth. There are all types of evils happening every where all over the world. The world as it stands today is infested with evils of all types. The Apostle John gave us the clear picture that the entire world is in wickedness.

1 John 5:19 "And we know that we are of God, and the whole world lieth in wickedness."

The evil one is going about causing evil and havoc in the lives of so many people all over the world. Evil is the devils' ministry. He is an evil being who delights only in doing evil. The word of God is clear on this. Jesus said concerning the Devil that he comes only to do evil.

John 10:10 "The thief cometh not, but for to steal, and to kill, and to destroy..."

The Devil is busy doing what he has to do and he is doing it with all of his ability. Peter tells us that he is going up and down from place to place looking for those whom he can do damage to.

1 Peter 5:8 "Be sober, be vigilant; because your adversary the devil, as a roaring lion walketh about seeking whom he may devour."

This is a fact fully established in the scriptures of truth: the evil one is going about in this world doing evil every where he goes. This is the truth, however, we do not have to keep talking about the evils that he is doing in the world. We are in the world but we are not of the world.

We do not belong to the Devil's scheme of things. We are of another order; we are heavenly beings on the earth and we are just here for now, as ambassadors for Christ. We are not to become mouth pieces for the Devil. We must not help the enemy to advertise his wickedness.

Instead of becoming the Devil's mouth piece we can choose to speak of what God is doing. It is important to know that Jn.10:10 does not only talk about the Devil and what he does but also of Jesus and of what He does, Jesus says of Himself that **"I am come that they might have life, and that they might have *it* more abundantly."** We need to get busy talking about Jesus and the life He came to give to us.

When we continue to talk about the evils in the world we become candidates of the evils of the world. You need to understand that your mouth is a spiritual magnet that pulls what you say towards you. That is one of the reasons why we do not need to continue talking about the evils of the world.

There are armed robberies in the world but you do not have to become the Devils mouth piece that advertises what he is doing. There are accidents that claim lives, but you do not need to continue talking about how accidents happened here and how accidents happened there, how lives were lost here and how lives where lost there.

There are ritual killings taking place from place to place as the enemy seeks to destroy human beings, but you do not need to be the one who always tells of the latest news of such wickedness in the country. People are being struck down by sicknesses and diseases but you are not to be the one announcing such bad news.

There are people falling into all kinds of calamities day by day but you and I do not need to be the ones carrying such information around with us. Yes these things are happening but we do not need to be talking about and advertising them. We must leave that to the Devil and his children to do. We have enough good news from the word of God to talk about all the days of our lives.

Actually the word of God calls upon us to talk about God and His mighty power that is at work on the earth, and not about the evils that the enemy is doing.

> **Psalm 145:9-12 "The LORD is good to all: and his tender mercies are over all his works. All thy works shall praise thee, O LORD; and thy saints shall bless thee. They shall speak of the glory of thy kingdom and talk of thy power; to make known to the sons of men his mighty acts, and the glorious majesty of his kingdom."**

As the saints of God, we are to be busy talking about the power of God and making His mighty acts known to the children of men all over the world. Our tongues should be busy declaring the awesome greatness of our God. When people come close to us they need to hear something from us that exalts God, and reflects His mighty power. This should characterize every member of the kingdom of God. The fact that we are seated with Christ in the heavenly places should make it easer for us to fill our mouths with the wonders of God and the great things that He is doing all over the world.

The secular news media will never tell you about the great things that God is doing in the world today, they will not tell you of the five thousand sinners who got saved in a great crusade last week, but they will tell you of the people who committed suicide. They will not tell you of the blind man who got healed in church, but they will tell you of the man who got blinded by whatever. They will not tell you of the mighty move of the Holy Spirit going on in the world today, no, they would rather tell you of the evils that the enemy is doing.

That is their job, to carry the news of what the Devil is doing, we are not to join them in that job, but to look down from God's heaven and see from that perspective and talk of God's mighty power and the great things that He is doing among men and women in the world today.

The world is filled with evil but when you look from your perspective as one seated in heavenly places with Christ, you see the glory of God and not the evils of the Devil. Your view depends on where you are looking from. If you are looking from the realms of God's glory you will see the majesty of His power and His mighty wonders that He is doing every day.

When King Uzziah died, Isaiah saw the Lord seated and lifted high in the Temple. It was not a very wonderful time in the natural but Isaiah heard the angels say something profound. They were not talking about how the king died and what killed him, but rather they were talking of the great power of God. They said that the earth was filled with the glory of the Lord.

> **Isaiah 6:1-3 "In the year that king Uzziah died I saw also the Lord sitting upon a throne, high and lifted up, and his train filled the temple. 2 Above it stood the seraphims: each one had six wings; with twain he covered his face, and with twain he covered his feet, and with twain he did fly. 3 And one cried unto another, and said, Holy, holy, holy, is the LORD of hosts: the whole earth is full of his glory."**

The King was dead but the angels were not talking about that sad news but their words focused on the fact that the earth was full of God's glory. It is likely that the people of the land were still mourning the death of their king, but the angels, the heavenly beings got busy talking about the glory of God. No wonder they are always surrounded by that heavy glory of God. What you talk about is attracted to you, whether negative or positive. It is sad that some Christians take delight in talking about the evils happening around them.

Satan is always very happy when children of God help him to talk about the things that he is doing among men and women of the world. You must watch what you say. **Do not help the enemy to carry his bad news from place to place**. You get what you say, so if you get what you do not want, it simply shows what you've been busy saying. Therefore: **SAY WHAT YOU WANT**. This is a principle that can not be broken.

The truth is that this principle works whether we know about it or not and whether we want to believe it or not. It is not a matter of what we want to believe or what we do not want to believe, this principle is eternally abiding and we do ourselves well to understand it and to work with it for our personal benefit.

ACTION PRAYERS

1. Father I thank you for giving me the power to control my entire life in Jesus name.
2. Like the Horse's life is controlled by the bits, I, also control the events of my life by my tongue so only what I say shall happen in Jesus name.
3. My life is moving forward in the mighty name of Jesus Christ.
4. I will not be stagnant in Jesus name.
5. My Destiny is being controlled by the power of the Holy Spirit in Jesus name.
6. My future is secured; I refuse every form of frustrations in Jesus name.
7. My health is getting better in Jesus name.
8. Every arrow of sickness against my life, be broken in Jesus name.
9. My tongue is a blessing to my life therefore I do not speak negative things in Jesus name.
10. Every spirit of negative confessions, of defeat and failure be broken off my destiny now in Jesus name.
11. No weapon formed against my life will prosper; therefore I command every evil work against my life to be forever smashed in Jesus name.
12. My life is blessed so I live above every type of curses in the mighty name of the Lord Jesus Christ.

CHAPTER 2

LITTLE HELM, MIGHTY SHIP

Looking further into the text under consideration we observe that it also tells us something about the helm used in ships.

James.3: 4-5 "…behold also the ships which though they be so great, and are driven of fierce winds, yet are they turned about with a very small helm, withersoeveer the governor listeth. Even so the tongue…"

We have already seen that God compares the tongue to the bit put on the horse's mouth, but there is something else that the tongue is compared to: **HELM**. Ships are large locomotive vessels, and of all the invented methods of transport, the ship is the biggest. You can not compare cars to ships for instance; the biggest ship is much bigger than the biggest airplane. Not only are ships large and great, their path of journey is the most difficult.

Cars and buses move on the land while planes fly in the air; cars can have bumps and rough roads to contend with, airplanes can have rough weather and turbulent clouds to contend with, but the hazards of a ships journey exceeds both. The turbulence of the sea coupled with fierce wind current combined, make a 'sea journey' a tough one.

I remember being with a friend who was a Naval official that is involved with operating on high sea with their ships. He told me how uneasy it was for people who board naval ships for the very first time. The turbulence of the sea often causes them to throw up. When non naval personnel get on such ships and they experience the effects of sea turbulence they are eager to get off the ship.

The wonderful thing is that despite the turbulence of the sea together with the violence of the fierce winds, the Captain of the ship is able to control the large vessel and to move it wherever he likes. In spite of the large size of the ship and the great degree of turbulence the captain is still able to control the ship. It is interesting to observe that the scriptures say that the Captain is able to turn the ship wherever he likes.

That is profound. The ship can not determine where it should go, the turbulence of the sea can not dictate the direction that the ship should go and the violent winds do not determine where the ship should go. No matter how heavy these forces are, the Captain is still the one to determine where the ship should go. He is in control; his decision determines where the entire ship ends up.

It is important to note that the captain does not give up control of the ship just because it is large or because the turbulence is much. The captain does not allow the degree of turbulence to overwhelm him to give up his control of the ship because he knows that there is an ordained way to take control of the danger posed by the difficult situation. How do you see the situations that you are facing right now? Do you see yourself as defeated and hopeless? Do you see your case as the worst among human beings? If Satan has told you that your case is the worst there is, I like you to know that that is the exact same thing the Devil tells many people. If he tells you that your case is the worst and then be sure that he is telling the same lie to so many other people, you can easily understand why the Bible calls him a liar and the father of lies.

John 8:44 "Ye are of *your* father the devil, and the lusts of your father ye will do. He was a murderer from the beginning, and abode not in the truth, because there is no truth in him. When he speaketh a lie, he speaketh of his own: for he is a liar, and the father of it."

The Devil's lies have affected many people so badly because they do not know any better. There are some people who have been so overwhelmed by the lies Satan has told them about the crises of life that they decided to call it quits. They feel they have more than their fair share of troubles, so they have to bring everything to an end by killing themselves.

For the others who do not get to the dangerous extent of killing themselves, they rather get to the extent of giving up the desire to work towards a solution. They feel that their efforts are not yielding any results so they give up and begin to merely drift along in life.

It does not matter where you are in life today and what you are going through, you do not need to give up, the fact that you are still alive is an indication that God is not through with you yet. As long as there is life there is hope, God still has an answer waiting for you, if you will only know what to do. God's plan for you has not ended and will not end until He has fulfilled all that He has planned for you. God has kept you alive for a divine reason and He is actively working on your behalf even if you think He has forsaken you.

Ecclesiastes 9:4 "For to him that is joined to all the living there is hope: for a living dog is better than a dead lion."

There is hope for you in the name of Jesus Christ the Son of the Living God. You will win in the name of Jesus Christ. Your enemies will not have the last word in your life in Jesus name. Be like the captain in the ship who does not give up in the face of the turbulence of the sea. Make up your mind that you are not going to go down but that you will go through victoriously by the power of God's faithfulness. His word is true and when you walk with His set principles you can be sure of having the victory. Make up your mind to say what you want, knowing that you will get what you say. You must learn to unleash the power of God through the right use of your tongue.

WHAT IS THE KEY?

How does the captain gain control of the large ship? It is not by crying and waiting for the change to happen in "the sweet by and by". It is not by wishing and wishing on end. It is not by just praying and praying and then talking negatively after the prayers, nor is it by folding his hands. Some people live their lives by wishing that things get better. That is a wrong way to live. **Nothing happens by itself, whatever happens is made to happen**. Nothing moves until it is moved. Life is not meant to be lived on the altar of chance and luck. Something needs to be done if anything meaningful will happen.

The only way the Captain controls the big ship, is by holding and turning the helm of the ship to the desired direction and concerning this the bible says, even so the tongue, even so the tongue, even so the tongue! The ship is very large yet the Captain is able to turn it wherever he likes by the right use of the helm. The sea may be so angry and raging with terrible turbulence, however, the captain is able to gain control and to lead the ship to where he desires by the right use of the helm.

The helm is the key to being able to turn the ship to wherever the captain desires it to go. It is important to note that the captain does not even need to call a meeting of the people in the ship to talk about the way out of the dilemma; he simply does the right thing, namely, **turning the helm to the desired direction**.

It is good to share your challenges with people but it is much more important to know that you can not share them with just any body. Some people talk to many people about their problems without being willing to do the things needed to cause a release of the desired victory. The captain will fail if he begins to run around those in the ship asking them what he should do to bring the ship under control. In the same way you can not win if you have the habit of running around people asking for advice when you are not willing to do the right thing yourself.

It does not always help to be talking to so many people about the challenges you are facing. They are also facing some challenges and looking for the way out. When you share your challenges with the right people they will move you forward but when you share them with the wrong people they will only hear about it but yet never add anything to you in the direction of the answer that you really need.

You can replace sharing your challenges with everybody with the simple act of doing the right thing. Use your tongue to gain control over the challenges of life. Use your tongue like the captain uses the helm, face up to your desired direction and use your tongue to move your life in that direction. The time you spend talking about your challenges to people, use it to release words of faith in the direction you want your life to go.

God deliberately compared the tongue to both the bit and the helm, so that those who cannot relate to the horse may relate to the ship; God does not want His people to be ignorant of this wonderful kingdom principle, so He had to use double illustration to make it clear. When Jesus wanted to add emphasis to His words, He often said, "verily verily I say unto you". In English this is wrong grammar but the idea is that what follows is very important and should be given the importance it deserves. The Holy Spirit had James use double illustration for the tongue, the bit in the horses' mouth and the helm in the ship so that we may not miss it, and I pray for you that you may not miss it in Jesus name.

YOUR LIFE IS GREAT

The ship is large and some of them are really very large. Some cargo ships are so large that they can carry much more than any airplane can carry. We are aware that some war ships are so large that they do not only carry military airplanes, but they even serve as mini-airports where war planes take off and land in times of great military operations. Some ships are indeed massive.

I want to draw your attention to the fact that your life and mine are also very large. You may be just four feet tall and skinny but be it known unto you that your life is great and big. You are a spirit with a soul and living in a body. You are much more than what you appear to be. You have spiritual life, you have a mental and emotional life, you have physical life, you have your financial life, you have your family life, you have your business life, you have your past life, you have your present life, you have your future life etc, you are greater than any ship.

Your life is greater than you think. Every human being is a complex entity with details that go far beyond what many of us can ever think. No human being is small, no matter how small they may look physically. God made us in His image and He is a mystery. **He can not be fully understood or explained and that element of mystery is imbedded in all human beings**. How true that is! That is why some people never cease to surprise you. When you thought you knew them inside out, just then they come out in a new way and do things you never thought they could ever do. Human beings are mysterious beings.

> **Genesis 1:26 "And God said, Let us make man in our image, after our likeness: and let them have dominion over the fish of the sea, and over   the fowl of the air, and over the cattle, and over all the earth, and over every creeping thing that creepeth upon the earth."**

There is a depth and a width to your personality that you may not understand and this is because you are greater than you think you really are. Some ships are great but you are greater than any ship. Your spirit, your soul, your body, your finances, your family and every other area of your life all combined together show the greatness of your life.

No matter how great ships are, they pass away some day and turn into scraps but as for you, you are an unending being. You'll exist forever. The ships are for a while but you are forever and ever, all ship will pass away but you will not pass away, you are an eternal being. You are greater than the greatest ship in the world. **God made you in His own image**. The journey of the ship through the sea is like the journey we humans are making in this present life. The turbulence of the sea coupled with the violence of the winds is a picture of troubles, tests and trials that come across us as we live our daily lives in this present evil world.

This world is full of troubles and crisis and no one is exempted from having these challenges. In Isaiah, God's word shows us that challenges are a part of our lives, they are not occurrences that may happen but they are things that happen as a normal part of the game. It is therefore impossible to live in this present world and never have any challenges.

> **Isaiah 43:1-2 "But now thus saith the LORD that created you, O Jacob, and him that formed thee, O Israel, Fear not: for I have redeemed thee, I have called *thee* by thy name; thou *art* mine. ² When thou passeth through the waters, I *will* be with thee; and through the rivers, they shall not overflow thee: when thou walkest through the fire, thou shalt not be burned; neither shall the flame kindle upon thee."**

Passing through the waters and walking through the fire is only a matter of time. There are no ifs and buts about them; they are programmed as part of the game of life. Life without any challenge whatsoever is not possible on this side of heaven.

However, when we pass through the waters and when we walk through the fire, God has committed Himself to ensure our safety. Just as the challenges are real, the total victory is also real and certain. The turbulent waves of the sea that the ship encounters are similar to the challenges of life. We need to learn how to control our lives in spite of the challenges we face, we need to understand the power of the tongue in overcoming the storms of life.

The Bible teaches that the Devil is the god of this world (II Cor. 4:4) and as a result he keeps injecting evil and wickedness into the world. The Devil is not god of those who belong to Jesus Christ because the Father has delivered us from the kingdom of darkness (See Col. 1:12-13), but since we live in this world we constantly come across the evil of our days and as pointed out earlier the right use of our tongues can manifest our exemption from these evils.

" Therefore whosoever heareth these sayings of mine, and doeth them, I will liken him unto a wise man, which built his house upon a rock: and the rain descended, and the floods come, and the WIND BLEW and beat upon that house, and it fell not; for it was founded upon a rock. And every one that heareth these saying of mine, and doeth them not, shall be likened unto a foolish man, which built his house upon the sand: and the rain descended, and the flood came, and the WINDS BLEW, and beat upon that house, and it fell and great was the fall of it" Matt. 7: 24-27.   (Emphasis mine)

In the above scripture our Lord revealed the result of not doing His word. There was an attack on the house built by the two men, the wise and the foolish. **There are no exceptions**. The rain, the flood and the wind come against the good and bad, the godly and the ungodly. However, the house of the wise stood the attack while the house of the foolish man collapsed. The wise man was a doer of the word while the foolish man was only a hearer, deceiving himself.

James 1:22 "But be ye doers of the word, and not hearers only deceiving your own selves".

The collapse of the house of the foolish can not be blamed on the storms. If it was caused by the storms then the house of the wise man would have also fallen down. Two believers may have the same situations in their lives yet one of them falls flat while the other stands strong. The one who failed can not blame his failure on the challenge, because the other believer had the same challenge yet refused to fail. You can

28

not blame your failure on your circumstances, you can not blame it on your mountains because everybody has their own mountains and yet many are making strides in spite of the challenges.

In this illustration, Jesus described trouble with three things: rain, wind and flood. Again it is important to realize that Jesus did not say "if the wind blow, if the floods come and if the rain falls". The wind WILL blow, the floods WILL come and the rain WILL fall, that is why He said in John 16:33 that in the world we SHALL have tribulation, **but He has won the victory for us**.

> **John 16:33 "These things I have spoken unto you, that in me ye might have peace. In the world ye shall have tribulation: but be of good cheer; I have overcome the world."**

Therefore defeat can not be blamed on the fact that there are tribulations. Jesus has overcome the enemy for us already, but we need to realize what we need to do to unleash the power of the Lord into our situations and see the victory He has purchased for us become a part of our experience. Our tongue is a vital key to gaining victory no matter the storm that comes across our way.

THE TONGUE, LIKE THE HELM

The fierce winds that ships have to contend with on sea is exactly a picture of the flood, the rain and the winds that we all have to contend with in this life; but just as the Captain is able to control the whole ship, we can control our whole life by the use of our tongue. What type of words are you allowing to come out from your mouth? Are you using your tongue rightly like the horse rider does with the bits?

Are you using your tongue the way the captain uses the helm to gain control over the large ship? What are you saying? What trend of words is most common with you? What type of words characterizes your talk? When you are conversing with others, what message do you carry with your words? What characterizes your words?

The Bible says, even so the tongue, even so the tongue, even so the tongue. You may say "man of God you do not know how serious my situation is, things have become very, very bad with me; my health, my finance, my business, my everything, things are very bad… "I declare unto you in the name above every name, the name of Jesus Christ the son of the living God, that God has put something in your hands to change your situation. No matter how fierce the wind is blowing, you can use your tongue to control it. No matter how heavy the flood is, you can use your tongue to gain control in the name of Jesus Christ our king.

You can replace the evil around you with good if you know how to rightly use your tongue the way God intended you to do. The good that you desire can be released upon your life through the use of your tongue.

> **Proverbs 12:14 "A man shall be satisfied with good by the fruit of his mouth: and the recompense of a man's hands shall be rendered unto him".**

God can cause you to be satisfied with good through the proper use of your tongue. There is a living treasure of good invested in you by the Lord through His holy word. When you learn to speak the word of God and mix it with faith in your heart you are on the path to being satisfied with the goodness of God. I see you enter a new realm of satisfaction by the use of your tongue in Jesus name.

FEAR NOT

Fear is a destabilizing force of evil. When people allow fear to take control of their hearts, they begin to lose sense of direction and will eventually lose control of the situation. The enemy tries all he can to cause fear in the lives of God's people because he knows that fear will cripple faith and erode any sense of confidence in the power of God to save and to intervene.

When Goliath of Gath came roaring against Saul and the armies of Israel, they could not stand against him because they allowed fear to take over. The great boasts of Goliath was not the real problem. The real problem was that they allowed themselves to become afraid of Goliath. When David came on the scene he heard the evil man roar in the same way but he refused to be afraid and that made the difference. Fear just like faith is a matter of choice and you and I can choose not to fear as the people of God.

1 Samuel 17:10-11 "And the Philistine said, I defy the armies of Israel this day; give me a man, that we may fight together. ¹¹ When Saul and all Israel heard those words of the Philistine, they were dismayed, and greatly afraid."

When Saul and his men became afraid they lost even the capacity to trust in the saving power of God. They gave up ground to the enemy. There was no difference in the roaring of Goliath before David came and when David came. The same type of boastful shouts from the same evil monster, but yet David refused to be afraid. That is a very vital key. That Saul and his men were fearful was their defeat, and David's bold faith was the key to his victory. Putting yourself in that situation will you say that you could have been like Saul or you would have been like David? Are you fear filled or faith filled? Have you learnt to walk by faith in the midst of the storm?

We must not allow ourselves to become afraid of the enemy for whatever reason. The storms of life can be controlled in spite of their high degree of turbulence, provided we do not allow the enemy to cause fear in our hearts.

Philippians 1:28 "And in nothing terrified by your adversaries: which is to them an evident token of perdition, but to you of salvation, and that of God."

If the captain of a ship becomes afraid to use the helm because he thinks the wind is too fierce, he endangers both himself and the entire ship, but if he undermines the seeming toughness of the wind and simply turns the little helm to the desired direction, his journey will continue as though there were no violent wind. **Do not be afraid because of the negative experiences you are having, use your tongue to proclaim what you want based on the ever faithful word of God and as you persistently use your tongue positively there will be a change in your experience.**

Like the bit is to the horse, and the helm to the ship, so is your tongue to your entire life. The bit controls the whole body of the horse, so your tongue controls your entire life, your health, your spiritual life, your finances etc.

The helm controls the ship despite its large size and the fierce opposing winds it has to contend with, in the same way your tongue controls your life's vastness and fierce opposing circumstances. It does not matter what fierce storms you are coming up against, God has put power in your tongue to make a great difference as you engage His unchanging word with the constructive use of your tongue.

Many of us do not realize the degree of power that God has put in our tongues. The power to determine what happens to us, the power to control our environment and our experiences; the power to set the pace for what is allowed around us is placed on our tongues by the Lord.

> **Proverbs 18:21 1 "Death and life are in the power of the tongue: and they that love it shall eat the fruit thereof."**

Death and life are in the power of the tongue, what a profound statement from the word of God. The word that can not lie, the word that is eternally settled in heaven gives this profound truth. Death and life are in the power of the tongue. The Hebrew word used in this verse for **power**, is the word **yad**, meaning, 'hand'. So death and life are in the hand of the tongue, it is therefore the tongue that determines what happens in the realms of death and life. Death can not operate without the permission of the tongue and in the same way; life can not function unless the tongue allows it to do so.

The tongue can stop or allow death. The tongue can stop or allow life to flow. Death or life, it is up to the tongue. Failure or success it is up to the tongue. If the tongue can control death, then other things are not a problem. Death is the ultimate evil that human beings have to deal with and if death is at the mercy of the tongue then nothing can operate outside the control of the tongue. Death and life are in the power or control of the tongue.

Will you allow death to have its way with you? Or will you allow life to be the order of the day around you? The choice is yours and you unleash your choice by the use of your tongue. You can release life or you can release death, you can hamper proper functioning of your life or you can release the forces of life and enjoy all that God has for you. You can decide that death can not operate around you by refusing to speak words of death.

When the ship continues to go the wrong direction it's not because the wind is too fierce but because the captain has refused to turn the helm in the right direction. Don't blame your failure on your circumstances; it is a product of your inability to use your tongue correctly. **Dare to use your tongue according to the standard of God's word and see if your life will not be changed. Dare to speak your desire into manifestation and see what the Lord will do for you**.

ACTION PRAYERS

1. The storms of life shall not spoil my destiny in Jesus name.
2. Every violent storm raging in the sea of my life, I command you to stop right now in Jesus name.
3. No matter the type of wind blowing around the ship of my life, I conquer them by the power of God in my tongue in Jesus name.
4. As the Captain of the ship of my life I surrender my ship to the full Lordship of Jesus Christ.
5. The ship of my life will never sink in the sea of life in Jesus name.
6. The ship of my life will arrive at my divine destiny in Jesus name.
7. My destiny is secured by the mighty power of God in Jesus name.
8. Any beast working under the sea of my life to capsize the ship of my life receive judgment by fire in Jesus name.
9. With my tongue I declare that my life is blessed and not cursed in Jesus name.
10. I overcome every storm of life by the power of God in my tongue in Jesus name.
11. My tongue is a blessing to my life in Jesus name.
12. Every area of my life is covered by the glory of God in Jesus name.

CHAPTER 3

YOU GET WHAT YOU SAY

Mk. 11:20-24 "And in the morning as they passed by, they saw the fig tree dried up from the roots. And Peter calling to remembrance saith unto him, Master, behold the fig tree which thou curseth is withered away. And Jesus answering saith unto them, have faith in God. For verily I say unto you whosoever shall say unto this mountain, be thou remove and be thou cast into the sea; and shall not doubt in his heart, but shall believe that those things which he saith shall come to pass, he shall have whatsoever he saith. Therefore I say unto you what things so ever ye desire, when ye pray, believe that ye receive them, and ye shall have them."

JESUS AND THE FIG TREE

There was joy every where, the crowd was moving towards the same direction, clothes and tree branches were being spread on the road down to Jerusalem, it was the moment of the triumphant entry of Jesus Christ into Jerusalem the city of David. As Jesus entered the city of Jerusalem, He headed for the "house of God", the temple; he looked round and examined all things in it. And now it was evening time, so Jesus with the twelve disciples later called apostles, went out of town spent the night in Bethany, a close town about two miles east of Jerusalem.

The next day Jesus and his team came back from Bethany to Jerusalem, Jesus being hungry at this time saw a fig tree along their way so He went to it hoping to get something to eat. The fig tree had leaves on it, it appeared so rich and wonderful but to the shock of Jesus; He discovered the fig tree had no fruits on it.

There are many Christians who are like this fig tree, outwardly they look so lively and spiritually rich, but if you get close to them you will find out that they have no 'figs'. God is not pleased with fruitless Christians; He wants us to bear fruits that will abide. For a Christian to be in the faith for many years and yet show no fruit is a waste of space and God does not like that. As a Christian, how fruitful are you? What fruits have you produced and what divine results are coming from your life for the advancement of the glory of God on the earth? God wants us to be fruitful and productive.

John 15:16 "Ye have not chosen me, but I have chosen you, and ordained you, that ye should go and bring forth fruit, and *that your fruit   should remain: that whatsoever ye shall ask of the Father in my name, he may give it you"*.

Jesus could not stand the hypocritical look of the fig tree so He cursed it. Jesus said to the fig tree "no man eats fruit of thee hereafter forever". The moment He made that statement He knew the job was done, He did not try to make it happen by physical efforts. He was confident that the power of God was instantly released through His word. Jesus had understanding about the great power of God in His tongue and so must we. When we come to understand the power in our tongues; we shall release the word and be very confident that it will come to pass. You and I need to get filled with the word of God to the point that we speak His word all the time and we shall see what we say come to pass by the power of God. Saying something and being certain that it will come to pass does not come about over night. Spiritual growth and the knowledge of the word is central to operating in this realm of creative power.

We need to be filled with the word to the point that we naturally expect our words spoken in faith to materialize by the power of God. Any one of us can get to that realm of speaking creative power by faith but it will take a continuous deliberate time of dwelling in the word.

The Lord Jesus Christ spoke the word; He said what He wanted to happen. For deceiving the Lord of glory, the fig tree was condemned; no man would eat fruit from it any more. **Observe that the Bible did not say that Jesus prayed that no man will eat fruit of that fig tree anymore**, He did not pray, He simply spoke. All prayers involve saying, but not all sayings are prayers; so Jesus said unto the fig tree "No man shall eat fruits of thee hereafter forever" Jesus did not organize a prayer meeting to deal with the fruitless fig tree. He simply spoke as an act of His faith and it came to pass.

I have nothing against organizing prayer meetings to deal with issues that need to be divinely resolved we all believe in the awesome power of prayers, but I like you to see that it is not always prayers that gets the job done. **Jesus did not pray He simply spoke**, He put His faith to work and unleashed the power of God to produce what He wanted and He got what He wanted.

Some of us have become so religious that we pray and pray and pray but end up saying nothing meaningful at the end of our prayers. You can pray all you like but what do you say after you have prayed? All prayers involve the use of words from our mouths but there are times that we are not called to pray but to simply say with great confidence what God would have us to say. Say it, believe it and see it comes to pass by the power of God.

It is time we all reach out for the great substance of God's word and His mighty power and see His might manifested in Jesus name. God has great things in store for His people, but we need to wake up and walk with God as He intends for us to.

God has no pleasure in bareness and emptiness. However, there are many Christians today who are simply chasing shadows. Their major concern is for that which is glamorous, they are fanfare oriented, they appear active in God's service, but the fact is that they are doing their own thing and not God's. These fanfare oriented believers like to do egocentric activities, their desire is for recognition, and as a result of this they do not really produce abiding fruits. Such 'fig tree' Christians stand the risk of being cut off from the body of Christ by God the Father Himself.

John 15:1-5 "I am the true vine, and my Father is the husbandman. ² Every branch in me that beareth not fruit he taketh away: and every branch that beareth fruit, he purgeth it, that it may bring forth more fruit. ³ Now ye are clean through the word which I have spoken unto you. ⁴ Abide in me, and I in you. As the branch cannot bear fruit of itself, except it abide in the vine; no more can ye, except ye abide in me. ⁵ I am the vine, ye are the branches: He that abideth in me, and I in him, the same bringeth forth much fruit: for without me ye can do nothing".

36

If we must remain useful to the agenda of God we must be fruitful and result oriented. We must become producers and not just occupiers of space. After Jesus had cursed the fig tree, His team proceeded to Jerusalem where He cleansed the temple which didn't need cleansing the previous day. Let me just quickly note this point; **that your heart was clean yesterday does not mean it is clean today**.

Therefore search your heart everyday, don't depend on yesterday's holiness. There are some precious believers who were living holy lives before but for what ever reasons they have taken things for granted and lost their guards. Holiness must be a daily and a continuous thing in our lives. Jesus wants us to live like He did and we need to make it our goal to ever please Him by the life that we live. After this temple cleaning, Jesus went out of the city, most likely back to Bethany, because it was evening time.

JESUS GOT WHAT HE SAID

The next day they passed by, they saw a wonderful sight. The disciples saw that the fig tree which Jesus cursed the previous day was now completely dried up from the roots to the leaves. This was a great shock to the disciples, but not to Jesus. He said what He wanted and He knew it had to work, so when it happened it was not a surprise to Him.

Do you really realize that many people who get so excited when great miracles happen do so from the standpoint of unbelief? I do not mean to imply that we should not be excited when we see the miracles of God happen around us, by all means we should be excited and very glad, but our excitement must be a faith rejoicing and not an unbelief type of excitement. This is the type of excitement that Peter had because he had no faith in the words that Jesus had spoken.

When Peter observed this miracle he called the Lord's attention to it, he said, "Master, behold, the fig tree which thou curseth is withered away". In response to Peter's unbelief, Jesus opened a very powerful revelation about the power of words, Jesus revealed that you will get what you say.

The first thing Jesus said was 'have faith in God' or as the original Greek puts it, 'have the faith of God', implying that Peter was in unbelief. Jesus was saying in effect, "you can do the same thing, the faith of God that you see me just operate is also available for you, you can also do the impossible, you can have what you want ...." when you walk in unbelief you don't really expect anything to happen so if it eventually does happen, you are shocked, but if you really walk in faith you will absolutely expect something to happen and when it does you are not shocked with a shock of "you mean it really happened?" You are rather shocked when it does not happen but when it does happen you will be filled with thanks to God whose faithfulness is unto many generations.

As a pastor I have been privileged to see many miracles performed by the Lord in meetings. I have seen the blind see, the lame walk, the deaf hear, the dumb speak, all made whole by the Lord Jesus Christ the wonderful Saviour and Lord. Every time these miracles happen, I am greatly excited and glad at the power of God at work among the people. However, my excitement is not due to surprise of unbelief but one of thanksgiving to God for doing what He has promised to do. In verses twenty three and twenty four, Jesus revealed the unfailing power of faith manifested in two ways. In verse twenty three the release of the power of faith is through 'saying' while in the next verse it is through 'praying' and these two are different. Look at verse twenty three closely and note the words emphasized.

> **Mark 11:23 "For verily I say unto you, That whosoever shall *SAY* unto this mountain, be thou removed, and be thou cast into the sea, and shall not doubt in his heart, but shall believe that those things which he *SAITH* shall come to pass, he shall have whatsoever he *SAITH*".** **(Emphasis mine)**

If you look closely, you'll discover that this scripture is not talking about getting things done through prayers. It is not teaching about how to bring what you desire to pass by praying. **There is no doubt that prayer is very important, in fact when we stop praying we start playing with death**. Prayer is of great importance, but in this verse of scripture Jesus is teaching something else, and I wonder how many Christians have really come to understand what our Lord was saying here. In the last part of the verse Jesus said, "He shall have whatever he saith," so you see that the avenue through which the individual receives what he desires is not by prayer but rather by saying.

YOU CAN HAVE WHAT YOU SAY

The words 'say' and 'saith' appear three times while the word, 'believe' comes up only once, and the word 'prayer' is absent. Our Lord was teaching that you can get your desires fulfilled by believing His word once and saying what you believe thrice. It is vital to believe in your heart that you will receive from God, it is crucial to believe God's word in your heart, it is important to believe in your heart that you will receive from God, it is crucial to believe deep down in your heart that your desire will come to pass; but unless you say it with your mouth you'll keep wishing all your life.

In fact, the saying is more important than the believing; Jesus said "...he shall have whatsoever he saith". This word 'whatsoever' is very crucial, and it means anything and everything. This is why many people are experiencing the things they do not want. The reason for such experiences is related to what they are saying. **Jesus did not say "he shall have whatsoever he wants or desires" but he shall have whatsoever he says**. And whether it is good or evil, he shall have whatsoever he says. Therefore your saying is a key that unlocks your life for an inflow of what you say.

As you read this book right now, maybe you are experiencing spiritual bankruptcy, sickness, poverty etc. If you take a moment to think about what you have been saying about your life, you'll really see that it is likely that you are receiving what you said. Jesus said "... he shall have whatsoever he says". There is definitely a link between your present experiences and what you have been saying.

Jesus said we shall have what we say. Many of us do not realize the power in our tongues and the effect of what we say on our lives and our general experiences. Careless words should not be allowed out of your mouth; you need to be sure that you are not setting yourself up for a negative future. What are you saying about your finances and your relationships? What are you saying about your challenges?

ACTION PRAYERS

1. I declare that I get what I say in the mighty name of Jesus Christ.

2. Every barren fig tree of my life and destiny I command you to wither in the mighty name of Jesus Christ.

3. Whatever is not working in my life receive fresh life in Jesus name.

4. My tongue declares only good things about my life and I have what I say in Jesus name.

5. Every negative word I have ever spoken about my life, I command you to be wiped out in Jesus name.

6. My tongue is a blessing to my life in Jesus name.

7. My life is fruitful in Jesus name.

8. No evil shall befall me in Jesus name.

9. My life is advancing more and more in Jesus name.

10. Whatever my hand touches shall prosper in Jesus name.

11. Whoever blesses me is blessed and whoever curses me is cursed in Jesus name.

12. I am covered by the blood of Jesus Christ and all is well in my life in Jesus name.

13. My faithful God is in charge of my life and he orders my steps in Jesus name.

14. My path is getting better and better in Jesus name.

15. The God of heaven is on my side no one can be against me and succeed.

16. When I open my mouth my enemies will keep silent in Jesus name.

17. Every evil assignment against my destiny be destroyed in Jesus name.

18 I am blessed. I allow no evil to come out of my mouth.

CHAPTER 4

THE DAVIDIC MODEL

The scriptures give us a clear example of saying what we want and getting what we say. This sample is very clear in the instance of David and Goliath. I call this the Davidic Model. When David decided to face Goliath and put an end to the shame that he brought upon the Israelites, **he said what he wanted and he got what he said**.

Saul and every other member of the army of Israel kept saying that Goliath was too great to be challenged; they kept saying that they could not withstand him. They kept saying that Goliath was unbeatable and as long as they kept saying that that was what they got. Their words of fear and unbelief kept them under the subjection of the enemy; you can say that the enemy had them exactly where he wanted them.

This is exactly what happens with many Christians, the enemy has them just where he wants them. They are busy saying the words that the enemy gives to them; they see things from the standpoint of the flesh and continue to magnify their problems and challenges. Do not allow the enemy to have you where he wants, but rather choose to be where God wants you to be and put the Devil where you want him to be and that is under your feet.

However, the moment David came on the scene, he had a different language, and his words were of a unique type. He refused to say the same words that all of the soldiers where saying. He chose to go the way of God, the way of faith, the way of positive verbalization. David came up with a new type of verbalization; he knew the power of having what you say so he immediately started to say what he wanted.

His type of words was a solid ground for divine intervention. He spoke from God's perspective. **David refused to talk about how great Goliath looked; he knew that if he used his mouth to magnify Goliath his faith would be dislocated**. Stop magnifying your problems otherwise you will dislocate your faith. David opened his mouth and proclaimed the ability of his God and the weakness of his enemy. He kept saying that God will deliver the enemy into his hands just like He delivered

41

the Lion and the Bear into his hand.

His language of faith never changed. He refused to say anything opposite before his brethren; before other soldiers and even before the king. He maintained the same kind of words, words of faith and power and at the end, he got what he said. God almighty delivered Goliath into his hand and he killed him; got rid of the shame and brought eternal praise and glory to the Lord God.

I challenge you to get into the word of God and develop a word of God based vocabulary and hold on to it with a tenacious grip. Yes, challenges will come to your faith, but you must never give in to doubt and unbelief. You need to maintain your ground and speak faith come rain; come sunshine; come hell or high water. This is a vital key to having what you say. Say and keep on saying it even when it does not make any sense to say it, still say it anyway. It sure did not make any sense in the natural for David to talk the way he did. How in the world could David, a very young man who was a civilian talk about killing the amazing Goliath, it did not make sense but David kept saying it anyway.

1 Samuel 17:34-37 "And David said unto Saul, Thy servant kept his father's sheep, and there came a lion, and a bear, and took a lamb out of the flock: [35] And I went out after him, and smote him, and delivered it out of his mouth: and when he arose against me, I caught *him* by his beard, and smote him, and slew him. [36] Thy servant slew both the lion and the bear: and this uncircumcised Philistine shall be as one of them, seeing he hath defied the armies of the living God. [37] David said moreover, The LORD that delivered me out of the paw of the lion, and out of the paw of the bear, he will deliver me out of the hand of this Philistine. And Saul said unto David, Go, and the LORD be with thee".

1 Samuel 17:45-51 "Then said David to the Philistine, Thou comest to me with a sword, and with a spear, and with a shield: but I come to thee in the name of the LORD of hosts, the God of the armies of Israel, whom thou hast defied. [46] This day will the LORD deliver thee into mine hand; and I will smite thee, and take thine head from thee; and I will give the carcasses of the host of the Philistines this day unto the fowls of the air, and to the wild

beasts of the earth; that all the earth may know that there is a God in Israel. ⁴⁷ And all this assembly shall know that the LORD saveth not with sword and spear: for the battle *is* the LORD'S, and he will give you into our hands. ⁴⁸ And it came to pass, when the Philistine arose, and came and drew nigh to meet David, that David hasted, and ran toward the army to meet the Philistine. ⁴⁹ And David put his hand in his bag, and took thence a stone, and slang *it*, and smote the Philistine in his forehead, that the stone sunk into his forehead; and he fell upon his face to the earth. ⁵⁰ So David prevailed over the Philistine with a sling and with a stone, and smote the Philistine, and slew him; but *there was* no sword in the hand of David. 51 Therefore David ran, and stood upon the Philistine, and took his sword, and drew it out of the sheath thereof, and slew him, and cut off his head therewith. And when the Philistines saw their champion was dead, they fled".

Instead of allowing himself to become intimidated by the great size of Goliath, David stood in faith and started to speak words of victory and power. He declared how great God is. His words were very clear and firm. He was going to kill Goliath by the power of God. His words left no one in doubt that he was confident of having the victory. David spoke of total victory; he spoke in Goliath's face and declared his victory. David never stopped speaking what he wanted.

He wanted to kill Goliath and that was what he kept saying. Even when it did not seem to make any sense he still kept on saying it. David was far away from Goliath when he first spoke about killing him by the power of God, and he never changed that language of victory. It was possible for David to have become fearful when he really got close to Goliath and actually saw his unusual size up close but he refused to waver in his language of faith. Peter had faith that He could walk on water when Jesus asked him to come to Him on the water, but as he was on the water and really began to see the violence of the waters he became afraid and started to sink.

Matthew 14:29-30 "And he said, Come. And when Peter was come down out of the ship, he walked on the water, to go to Jesus. ³⁰ But when he saw the wind boisterous, he was afraid and beginning to sink. He cried, saying, Lord, save me."

43

Peter's faith was affected by the reality of the waves he had to confront but David stood fast and firm in the very face of Goliath Himself. David said what he wanted and he got what he said. You and I can also get what we say if we learn to operate the Davidic model of victorious faith confessions. God has loaded our tongues with His power, so when we speak, a path is charted for those words to come to pass.

To some Christians their problem is not exactly the issue of prayerlessness, they have no trouble with prayers but their problem is with 'the saying side' of their lives. **When you want to pray as a Christian it is quite easy to put on your pious garments of religiosity and pray some sanctimonious prayers that appears very religious but when you've done praying, what do you say**. Take it this way, what do you say in between your times of prayers.

Many Christians **'pray right but say wrong'**. They pray faith but say unbelief. They pray boldness but thereafter speak fear. They pray abundance and then turn around and speak lack. They pray power and then talk weakness. They pray victory and when they finish praying they start to talk defeat. Some people pray success and then when they are through they start to talk failure. What are you saying, that's exactly what you are going to get. Our Lord said, "… he shall have whatsoever he saith".

SAY WHAT YOU DESIRE

Since you know that you'll get what you say, then I suggest you better begin to say what you want, instead of crying, complaining and talking about what you do not want, focus on what you do want and keep saying it in the name of the Lord Jesus Christ and you'll receive a harvest of what you need. You can learn to say what you want even when it does not seem to make any sense in the natural. It made no sense for David to be talking about killing Goliath but because that was what he wanted he kept on saying it. Do you want to be healed? Then speak healing to your body.

Say to your body "in the name of Jesus I am healed. My body is the temple of the Holy Spirit, not for sickness. I am healed by the stripes of Jesus Christ" whether you feel pains or not has nothing to do with it, keep saying it because you'll get what you say.

Focus your attention on talking about the healing that Jesus purchased for you on the cross rather than talking all day about the sickness that the Devil is attacking your body with. Talk about your strength in the Lord and not your weakness in your self. God does not like you and I to continue speaking about sickness and disease when Jesus has paid the price to give us perfect health.

I am not implying that there will be no times when the enemy will try to put sickness on us, he will surely try to do that, because he is very stubborn and adventurous, but you need to become more stubborn than the enemy himself. Stand on the word and continue to talk about your healing or whatever it is that you are believing God for.

God wants us to cut off the word "sickness" from our language. We can begin to live the future life of glory here on earth now. This is a vital meaning of "thy kingdom come".

> **Isaiah 33:24 "And the inhabitant shall not say, I am sick: the people that dwell therein *shall* be forgiven *their* iniquity".**

Sickness is not a part of our redemption, therefore we need to learn how to say a big no to it all the time and when we really say no to it we shall refuse to preoccupy ourselves with talking about it, no matter how we feel in our bodies. We need to learn to say the right things, things that make for faith and victory in Jesus Christ.

The inhabitants of that glorious coming kingdom shall not say I am sick; they shall put away such words from their vocabulary. Somebody may say that this blessing is for the millennium when our Lord shall physically reign on the earth for one thousand years. This is true but we can and should live the type of life here on earth today and now.

One of the features of that coming glorious era is that our sins shall be forgiven and since our sins are forgiven now, why can't we live like those whose sins have been forgiven. The righteous are to put away sickness from their language. I also believe that the righteous are to put away failure and lack and all negatives from their vocabulary. We are to say what the word of God says. Now if the righteous will not say that they are sick then they must learn to say something else. The Bible actually demands that the weak say they are strong.

Joel 3:10 "Beat your plowshares into swords, and your pruning hooks into spears: let the weak say, I *am* strong."

It is natural for the weak to say that they are weak. God is not natural, He is supernatural in His way of doing things. God operates in a different way. Even though the weak feels weak, God expects them to say they are strong. God knows what He put into our tongues, He knows the awesome power in our tongues. He knows that if we continue to say how weak we are we shall only get weaker and weaker. If the weak keep on saying they are weak, then they will remain weak, but as they begin to say that they are strong, then they will become strong because they will have what they say. Stop talking sickness and disease and instead talk health and healing. Jesus paid the price for you and I on the cross. He took our sicknesses and diseases on Himself; therefore we have the redemptive right to perfect soundness.

If you want financial miracles to meet your needs, then say "My God supplies all my needs in the mighty name of Jesus, I am faithful to God with my tithes and offerings and seeds; the Lord is my shepherd I do not want ...." As you say this again and again and again, you'll have what you say. Jesus said "he shall have whatsoever he says". Say what you want. Stop talking about how your finances are bad and nothing good is happening, say what you want, and say what the word of God says.

It is clear that you have to be a faithful giver and tither before you can boldly call yourself a tither and a giver. Otherwise your faith will not work.

What are you saying today? Take note of them because that's what you will receive tomorrow. Jesus said "fig tree you are finished, no man shall eat of you any more" and Jesus got exactly what He said and so shall we. Unfortunately, however, some people are offending and wounding themselves with their own tongue, they are ever so busy saying things they have no business saying. James said something about the offending use of the tongue.
    "For in many things we offend all, if any man offend not in word,

not for the grace of God that opened the eyes of the pastor, she would have lost her child. How many people have lost their inheritance and their blessings to the enemy because of the wrong use of their tongues? You have what you say, therefore it is important that you refrain from dwelling on things you do not want.

Are you offending your spiritual life with your own words? When you say "Prayer is so hard for me, I can't pray for more than one hour at once; this world is so full of sin to the extent that to live holy is so difficult… "You are offending your spiritual life, with your mouth, you are creating a lousy spiritual life for yourself and that is going to be your experience.

You offend your own marriage when you say things like "my husband is a very selfish and wicked man, he does not love me at all, I am unfortunate to have married him…" or as a man you may say "my wife is a useless woman, she is very lazy and heartless…" Such words are offensive to your marriage because they are going to produce evil in your relationship. If you continue to say negative things about your children you are going to reap what you sow.

Many times people blame their spouses for troubles they are facing whereas they are the ones offending and wounding their marriages by their wrong use of words. It is important that you use words carefully because you are going to get what you say, **therefore say what you want**.

ACTION PRAYERS

1. You evil Goliath against my life, this very day I prophesy your death in Jesus name.
2. Like David I out-speak my Goliaths in Jesus name.
3. In my life, Goliath shall never have the last say in Jesus name.
4. You Goliath operating against my destiny, you come against me with your wickedness but I come against you in the mighty name of the Lord Jesus Christ.
5. No Goliath shall overcome me in Jesus name.
6. You Goliath of failure and defeat I declare that this very day the Lord will deliver you into my hands in Jesus name.
7. Every Philistine force backing up Goliath against my life today you shall all be destroyed in Jesus name.
8. You Goliath of bad luck and set back be destroyed by fire in Jesus name.
9. You Goliath of sin you shall never prevail in my life in Jesus name.
10. You Goliath coming against me from my family background, what are you still waiting for, be destroyed by fire in Jesus name.
11. Lord strengthen my tongue against every Goliath in Jesus name.
12. I have what I say and I say every Goliath standing on my way is delivered into my hands by the power of God in Jesus name.

CHAPTER 5

THE TONGUE IS A FIRE

The bible teaches that the tongue is a fire and the earlier we understand that, the better for us. The tongue has the capacity to set lives on fire. This is a fundamental truth that is very clear from the word of God.

"And the tongue is a fire, a world of iniquity; so is the tongue among our members, that it defileth the whole body and sendeth on fire the course of nature, and it is set on fire of hell". (James 3:6).

TONGUES OF FIRE

This scripture declares that the tongue is a fire, a world of iniquity and because of that it sets on the fire of hell and defiles the whole life with iniquity. This evil fire manifests in all forms of destructions and devastations. This is the negative side of the tongue, but we need to realize that there is a positive side to fire as well.

Not all fire is hellish and evil and not all worlds are of iniquity. In fact concerning fire, the bible says that "our God is a consuming fire". Heb. 12:29 therefore there is the fire of God and the fire of Heaven. This accounts for the positive fire, the fire that is good to us and nothing but good. The fire of God is real and that fire can operate through our tongues. This is why on the day of Pentecost the fire of God came upon the saints in the form of tongues.

"And there appeared unto them cloven tongues like as of fire, and it sat upon each of them". (Acts 2:3)

James talks about the tongue being a fire of evil and hell, but in Acts 2:3, God presents to us tongues like fire, in other words tongues with the fire of the Holy Spirit. The mighty fire of God came upon every believer in the upper room on the great day of Pentecost and what a great experience that was for all of those precious saints. God wants us to be on fire and more exactly He wants our tongues to be on fire for His praise and glory.

He placed one tongue of fire on each person- One person, one tongue of fire. Why did God not put more than one tongue on each person? I believe God gave each of them one tongue because God did not design anybody to have two tongues. **Even though some people talk and talk and talk as if they have more than one tongue the basic truth is that God gave each of us only one tongue.**

Too much pointless talk constitutes a spiritual liability. One tongue is enough otherwise God may have put more than one tongue of fire on some of the people in the upper room. If you want to keep yourself out of the path of trouble you need to avoid parroting. There is great wisdom in being a person of few words. **Speak only when necessary and keep quiet when you have to do so.** Even a fool who reduces the amount of words he speaks is assumed to be a wise person.

Proverbs 17:28 – "Even a fool, when he holdeth his peace, is counted wise: *and* he that shutteth his lips *is esteemed* a man of understanding".

It is wise for you to watch the words you speak and it is a fact that the fewer the words the easier it is to manage them well. The bible advices us to be quick to hear, but slow to speak.

James 1:19 "Wherefore, my beloved brethren, let every man be swift to hear, slow to speak, slow to wrath."

It is therefore not wise to be a talkative.

WHAT KIND OF FIRE?

The tongue is a fire, but the kind of fire produced by your tongue depends on you; you have to choose either the fire of hell or the fire of the mighty Holy Spirit. Negative fire from your tongue, defiles the whole body and sets the whole life on the fire of hell; producing sin, sickness, diseases, weakness, failure, poverty, restlessness, defeat and discouragement and all other things that resemble hell.

When, however, you choose that your tongue will be a tongue releasing the positive fire then that is what you will get. If your tongue is one of positive fire, it will produce healing, divine health, freedom from sin, total holiness, victory, breakthroughs, joy, peace and all other things that resemble life in heaven where the God of fire dwells.

Which is your choice, Satan's fire or God's fire? When you speak evil and negative things that amounts to saying what Satan is saying. When you speak sickness and disease you are saying what the Devil is saying. If you speak failure and defeat, you are speaking what the enemy is speaking. If you speak sin and perverse words, you are talking after the order of the Devil and with all that type of words you are using your tongue to produce the wrong kind of fire, you are using your tongue to unleash a negative kind of fire.

However, if you choose to speak ONLY the word of God and add to God's word exactly what you want (in line with God's will) your tongue is releasing the fire of God and the result will be joy, strength, victory, healing, peace, prosperity, holiness of heart and life and whatever you want from God.

Choose the fire of God, start to speak what the word of God says, focus on the word of God and keep on saying it with great faith and boldness. Step away from the realms of negativity and enter into the realms of God and His holy word. Keep a watch over your mouth and speak the word of God only, fill your heart with the word of God and speak it out concerning all the areas of your life, no matter what you are seeing with your physical eyes. No matter what you are hearing with your physical ears, no matter what you are feeling in your body, stand on the word of God and speak His word and your own word in line with His, and you shall have what you say.

In the name of Jesus Christ the Son of the Living God, I challenge you to stop complaining and murmuring about things going wrong in your life. Stop saying what you don't want because you'll get what you say therefore **say what you want in the name of the Lord Jesus Christ. It is well with you in Jesus name**.

WHAT SHOULD YOU SAY?

We are expected to speak words that are in agreement with the word of

God. If God says something, we are to say the same thing and adapt it to our particular situation without contravening His clear will.

God is a speaking God and so like Him we need to be a speaking people. Now this looks like a contradiction to what we have been saying about avoiding a life style of parroting. When you look at the word of God you will find that God often spoke things into manifestation before He actually did those things. Before Jesus came He kept saying it and saying it for hundreds of years and at last the Lord Jesus came just as God said He would.

In the story of creation, we know that God had to personally speak the elements of nature into existence before they actually manifested in the physical. That is the way it works. On the other hand parroting is mouthing unnecessary words just for the sake of talking.

The type of talking that God had in mind for us to be involved in makes room for His will to be brought into manifestation in the lives of His people. Saying what you want is saying what God is saying. So how do you know what God is saying? We need to go into the word of God if we must know what God is saying. God is a speaking God and so we must make our speaking meaningful and centered on the word of God.

God has given us precedence in His word that makes it clear that He wants us to speak His word in our own lives and situations. Consider how Paul portrayed this idea in the book of Hebrews.

> **Hebrews 13:5-6 "Let *your* conversation *be* without covetousness; *and be* content with such things as ye have: for he hath said, I will never leave thee, nor forsake thee. 6 So that we may boldly say, The Lord *is* my helper, and I will not fear what man shall do unto me."**

Our conversation or our lifestyle is to be without covetousness as the children of God. He is able and willing to take care of His own. Our avoidance of covetousness is partly caused by what God has said. However, what God said does not only make us put on a positive lifestyle, it also makes us speak. We are to say something because God has said something.

Our speaking is based on what God said, God spoke and so we also speak. This is the matter and this is how it works. Actually Paul wrote that "He said… so that we may boldly say…" God has spoken so we also may speak and we do speak in line with what God said. **We do not only have to say what God said in terms of language and choice of words but we are to add our own words to His words provided we do not contradict what He said**.

The bible said **"for he hath said, I will never leave thee, nor forsake thee"** so we see here that God said " I will never leave thee nor forsake thee" God has promised that He is personally present with us and as a result we are to say our own words in line with what God said. It is important to observe that we are not necessarily to say that "God is with us and will never leave us" we can and should say that but it is important to observe that we are called to say our own words that are in line with what God has said. He said He will never leave us nor forsake us.

So that we may boldly say, The Lord is my helper, and I will not fear what man shall do unto me. Based on the fact that God is with us and will not forsake us then we can say "the Lord is my helper and so I will not fear what man shall do unto me". It is important to see the fact that God wants us to speak His word and our own words in line with His. God has said so that we may boldly say. **So one of the reasons why God speaks to us is to empower us to speak**. He speaks among other things to give us the basis to speak; God's word is our motivation to speak.

We are therefore to open our mouths and speak the word of God with great boldness based on what God has said. Therefore because God has said, no weapon fashioned against us shall prosper we have the reason to speak also.

> **Isaiah 54:17 "No weapon that is formed against thee shall prosper; and every tongue *that* shall rise against thee in judgment thou shalt condemn. This *is* the heritage of the servants of the LORD, and their righteousness *is* of me, saith the LORD."**

We can boldly say "we are totally victorious over all the power of the enemy and no weapon can prosper against us. No matter the attack that comes on us, we will always win in Jesus name…."

Since God has said that by the stripes of Jesus we are healed, we have basis for speaking along the lines of healing and health.

Isaiah 53:3-5 "He is despised and rejected of men; a man of sorrows, and acquainted with grief: and we hid as it were *our* faces from him; he was despised, and we esteemed him not. 4 Surely he hath borne our griefs, and carried our sorrows: yet we did esteem him stricken, smitten of God, and afflicted. 5 But he *was* wounded for our transgressions, *he was* bruised for our iniquities: the chastisement of our peace *was* upon him; and with his stripes we are healed."

1 Peter 2:24 "Who his own self bare our sins in his own body on the tree that we, being dead to sins, should live unto righteousness: by whose stripes ye were healed."

We can boldly say "In Jesus name, we are healed and free from the power of sickness and diseases. Jesus paid the price and so we are healed by His stripes and free from sickness in Jesus name. Sickness can not tie us down; we are free to enjoy divine health…."

Based on the fact that God said that whatever we do shall prosper, we can boldly say "we are blessed and we are making progress in life. We are increasing and it is well with us, what ever we touch becomes a success. We do not fail, we prosper in all our ways…"As you continue to speak the word of God and add your own words in line with it and maintain your positive confession of faith, God will see to it that you have what you say. It is time to deliberately begin to speak the things you want into existence, stop saying the things you do not want and start to say what you want.

ACTION PRAYERS

1. My tongue is full of the Holy Ghost fire; therefore I command every evil against my life to be burnt in the name of Jesus.
2. Every evil fire operating against me, be consumed by the fire of the Holy Spirit in Jesus name.
3. My destiny is covered by the fire of the Holy Spirit therefore every

evil finger pointing against my destiny be consumed in Jesus name.

4. My health is getting better in Jesus name.

5. My finance is getting better in Jesus name.

6. My family is blessed in Jesus name.

7. I declare that my progress shall move in double speed in Jesus name.

8. The works of my hands are blessed and so whatever I do prospers in the mighty name of Jesus Christ.

9. Whatever I bless is blessed and whatever I curse is cursed in Jesus name.

10. My tongue shall never work against me again in Jesus name.

11. I command my tongue to work in my favour in Jesus name.

12. My belly shall be satisfied by the fruit of my mouth in Jesus name.

13. Whatever I say comes to pass, so I say that I am moving forward in all areas of my life in Jesus name.

14. Every stagnant areas of my life receive the fire of the Holy Spirit in Jesus name.

15. With my tongue I clear every obstacle on my way in Jesus name.

16. With my tongue, I clear every barrier against my increase in Jesus name.

17. My tongue is anointed to rule therefore I say that I rule over my enemies in the mighty name of Jesus Christ.

18. From today, my tongue shall never alter any negative thing about my life in Jesus name.

19. With boldness I declare that I shall have what I say and so I shall always say what I want in Jesus name.

20. My destiny is very colourful and it shall become more and more colourful every day in the mighty name of Jesus Christ.

THIS IS THE DAY OF SALVATION

God loves you more than you can imagine. His great love made Him sacrifice His only begotten son for your salvation. (John 3:16). God has no pleasure in your death, He wants to save you and lavish you with the riches of His great love and grace.

Now is the time to experience God's saving grace. There is room for you in God's kingdom; you can come in today; NOW. Tomorrow is not guaranteed, you need to do it today and this very moment is the best time that you have.

To be saved you may pray the following words.

"Heavenly Father, I repent of my sin, I accept Jesus Christ as my Lord and personal Savior. I believe Jesus died for me. Heavenly Father save me from my sins now in Jesus' name. From this moment I confess that Jesus is the Lord of my life and I will serve Him forever and ever, amen".

As you have prayed this prayer Jesus has saved you. Welcome into the family of God. Contact us for further assistance in your new life of faith in Christ and we shall help you with some resources that will help you move to the next level in your walk with the Lord Jesus Christ. God bless you and all that is yours in Jesus name. Your time to be celebrated has come. Your Time Has Come!

RESPONSE!

If this book has been a blessing to you and you may like to contact us, please see below:

Pastor Alex Omokudu
Victorious Pentecostal Assembly (VPA)
19-21 Thames Rd
Barking, Essex
London IG11 0HN
Website: www.vpa-tv.org
Email: vpacanaanland@yahoo.co.uk, vpateam@googlemail.com
Phone: +447903799998, +447535330808.

My Study Notes

My Study Notes

My Study Notes

OUT NOW

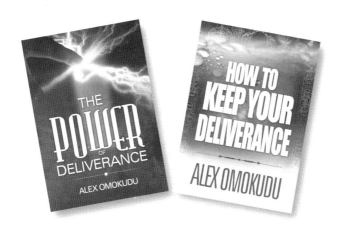

• THE POWER OF DELIVERANCE
• HOW TO KEEP YOUR DELIVERANCE

By

Pastor Alex Omokudu

Get your own copies of the two part series entitled The Power of Deliverance and How to keep your deliverance. These books address the subject of deliverance in careful detail; resolving much of the questions that had been unanswered in the minds of many believers. You are equipped with a deeper understanding for the importance of deliverance and most importantly how to keep the deliverance you have secured. Do not miss out on your own copies now!

To order a copy, Please call
Telephone: + 44 (0) 208 594 1444, +44 (0) 208 594 3434
Mobile: +44 (0) 7903 799 998
E-mail: vpacanaanland@yahoo.co.uk, vpateam@ googlemail.com
You can also send us your address and payment
so that we may post it to you.

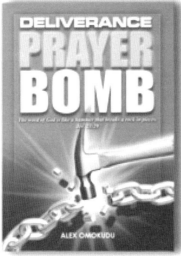

DELIVERANCE PRAYER BOMB

By

Pastor Alex Omokudu

This power packed book is a must read for everyone that seeks a colourful destiny.

I have carefully compiled it for you to pray with at all times. I encourage you all to have a copy and send it to your friends and families.

The prayers in it were the same set of prayers that made me a strong man of God. It covers all facets of human problems and the book is backed up with striking bible passages.

To order a copy, Please call
Telephone: + 44 (0) 208 594 1444,   +44 (0) 208 594 3434
Mobile: +44 (0) 7903 799 998
E-mail: vpacanaanland@yahoo.co.uk, vpateam@ googlemail.com

You can also send us your address and payment
so that we may post it to you.